Love, Depression, and Other Things Hollywood Romanticizes

ISBN: 9781702721783

Dedication

For my Meemee,

the most precious angel in heaven,

who gave me my love of music and writing

And to the people who inspired this book

who will never read nor would want to

because you're in it

Meet you in hell.

Contents

Acknowledgement

This poetry book would not have been possible without the encouragement and pleasure of knowing my friends, family, and all my exes. Thank you for the laughter, joy, and misery that gave this poetry book life.

I want to give special thanks to my boyfriend, Alex, and best friend, Megan Prendergast, for helping beat back the demons inside my mind in order to actually publish this book as well as convince me maybe I had something to say. I don't think I would be doing a lot of the things I'm trying to do without their support and I will always be grateful we all met.

And of course, to my dear Meemee, for all your unconditional love and support. I hope we meet again.

LDR

If home is where the heart is,

I have never been home.

My world has been reduced to numbers and measurements:

.4mm of a glass screen,

1 hr 6 min and 36 secs for our last phone call,

(3.1 mega pixels) X (the number of flower pictures   you
send every morning)

                                        To enjoy with my 1,189.4
mi away breakfast,

                                For the last 5 years.

If home is where the heart is,

I have never been home.

There is no i in me

I'm living life in decaf coffee,

Stacked in ounces of baby carrots

And cotton balls soaked in OJ

Settling in the stomach.

It's satin, silk, and rotting beef.

I still hear mooing in the halls.

I have to puke until they believe.

We're serving ice cream a la mode.

Anxiety (Is as dramatic as it seems)

Used knives, an illusion, I unwittingly unsheathed.

Panic\ Panic\ I have no air to tell you.

My lungs are closing up; I cannot breathe.

It's eaten away, comrades of the same disease,

Façades of honeysuckle and honeydew.

Used knives, an illusion, I unwittingly unsheathed.

Spectre boils and warts and stretch marks seethe,

Waking hours, wounded alarm clock howls, déjà vu,

My lungs are closing up and I cannot breathe...

Each new splintered coffin, too apathetic to grieve.

Lifespan within a silver skeleton keyhole view,

Used knives, an illusion, I unwittingly unsheathed,

It slices logic with marksman expertise[

When did I carve these misshapen scar tattoos?/

My lungs are closing... up and I cannot... breath^

I cannot breathe+ I cannot breathe= Help me# A vacuumed plea\

Panic/ Panic/ It's filling my lungs[festering pitch mildew/

Used knives" an illusion[I unwittingly unsheathed{

My lungs are closing up_ I cannot breathe

Depression is when

Church bells toll and you don't think of Weddings.

Or of veils, and coat tails and "I dos."

Champagne, bubbly Mary Janes jumping to catch the bride's bouquet.

I hear the Bell bellow and it hollows the chronic migraine in my chest.

I hear the solid knocking of wood at a funeral,

Creaking all 6ft down.

Heavenly Bodies

My nose is earth,

My eyes, mars and mercury,

My kisses, Venus.

The tail of your comet has freezer-singed my skin supernova,

Crashing through the atmosphere,

Cratering the core of my lonely planet.

We are dust on the mantle,

made of star stuff

reflected through the innocent

wonder of a child's eyes.

Gazing up in our small house,

At our tiny tendon of the universe.

Requiem for a Pansy

I threw a coin in the fountain,

Wrought by its own iron.

The pretty penny glinted in copper,

With no wish because my wish was you.

I'm the purple pansy someone tossed in

earlier that morning.

I happened to see myself while drinking Chai tea,

Fresh from powder at Fountain City Coffee.

My yellow face drinks in my

unquenched thirst.

My petals lap at the water

but I couldn't drink without my

roots and without my

roots I couldn't push up to gasp in air,

to breathe.

I drowned in that iodized water.

The ripples strummed my requiem in C#,

And though it deafened me

Through the honks and beeps,

No one on the busy street,

Heard a sound.

Art imitates life

No, art mocks life.

Duchamp was right

Life is stamped with R. Mutt

In black on the urinal rim

with kosher salt

And a different kind of lime,

Selling what is obviously not a

Margarita...

As a Margarita.

Life mocks art.

We deem art worthy by the

Nature

In Which we make

Up

The loneliness of the

Black dot surrounded by white

Canvas.

"A criticism of capitalism"

Or

"Consumer culture"

Or

"A satire of political satires"

$1,000,000

To be hung

18

And never touched.

God mocks life.

He gave me the gift of gab

In a dying art.

I mean,

Who really reads poetry anyway?

Prince Paradox

He was a paradox wrapped in a riddle served on a wooden plate.

She was a cupcake wearing a studded leather jacket with an arsenic filling

leaning on the wall of a whore house.

They met at the swell of the sea.

The foam teasing The Lorelei; its slick edifice,

soaked and rigid.

"Don't be fooled by the frosting."

"Frosting alone is too sweet. It is the mix and contrast that are best."

He consumed her.

20

She was the rogue, Dear Prince,

But you would still have tea with her.

Earl Grey and Irish Breakfast,

Tea time for two,

With a man who admires her well-formed ankles,

With a woman who licks buttercream frosting from his fingertips

but

still

blushes

at the tender kisses

He provided.

She was as accustomed

To them as the way you are accustomed

To gas station hard-boiled eggs for breakfast.

Richard Cory, I Understand

Richard Cory, one calm summer night,

Went home and put a bullet through his head.

And in this poetic elegy I write,

I wish I could have taken his place instead.

I smile in moments like my middle sister with a blue sugar spun giraffe,

But I ping pong as Sleepless Beauty in my bed,

Scraped up every last contented sigh and laugh,

But all that glitters is gunshot dead.

Being richer than a king isn't air

20,000 leagues under the sea.

We flutter pulses; We learn to wear a face.

Bury Meemee's pearls and Aunt Francis's doily lace.

My littlest sister gets up every morning to make me coffee,

So why do I envy Richard Cory that one calm summer night?

My mind twists and curls around the stark petal of a lily.

I find Richard Cory lucky.

He got relief.

High Hopes

The sky rusted over,

there wasn't enough WD-40 to keep the clouds rolling.

So I stay in the same field,

with the same wildflowers,

My skin peppered with daisies,

Letting the ants crawl up and bite my arms as a warning.

I don't write the tragedies, I live them.

I sympathize with both the fox and the rabbit,

Chasing each other's tails, Until they're worn plumb out barely
resting between each duel dance of yin and yang.

Keats,

your name may be writ in water,

but at least it was writ at all.

Love is War

The article was useless.

Her name still flashed on your phone screen,

And I was still left to lick sandpaper across what was left of a mahogany table,

already straining against 5 years of rot.

But Love is war,

And...

The only clip I had in my magazine was to keep my page

In Cosmopolitan:

"How to Please Your Man."

Color Theory

I am purple

And the entire spectrum of color is the distance between us

It's been blue living in the red.

I'm green at the star-crossed lovers, too yellow-bellied to admit

That I hate romance movies not

Because I'm an edge-lord but

Because the silver screen lies.

I've felt orange streams of sunset swirl, unfurl and claw through my
night's stomach,

Fading ombré to the stars,

Leaving droplets of constellations on my lashes.

I'm still in the drizzle before the rainbow but I know

My umbrella will keep me company.

Plunk

Plunk, plunk, plunk, plunk;

Discord across the barnacled driftwood,

slabs pirates would force you to walk.

If only they could make you jump.

The fog is impenetrable, and in the beginning,

there was still no set horizon.

But we are unable to spare the 50 cents for a far viewer.

Only the barnacled driftwood, weak and splintered, keeps me from

Exploring the turbulent waters involuntarily. But perhaps,

The slurry is an illusion just like the horizon.

The sea is quick to give us salty kisses

or salty tears dragged

up from its abyss depths

Previously overcast by the surface.

Anti-treasures you had hoped were lost and forgotten.

The grey is pierced by light.

It returns in

slow, steady cycles.

You reach out your hand as far as your

fingers can stretch...

... Did you miss it? Or is it possible it is

impossible to capture like

A laser pointer's beam?

Uncatchable even by the

quicker

cat?

Because of You

I noticed the glitter in the concrete like stars in a grey, hapless galaxy,

Thrust in an uncaring universe and it stubbornly "uncares" right back.

You received my first love poem in pink ink on a postcard

Along with gingersnap cookies that sparked thoughts of sugarplums.

I had my empty hand reach out and be met with yours.

Pixel bouquets, virtual hair-holding when I puke, digital breakfasts set out

by you with my favorite tea: Earl Grey.

But, really, you don't want me.

I've waited hours anxious and bleeding out for a single text.

The gifts you've sent are to stave off a bitch in heat;

Dildos and butt plugs don't stopple endless voids.

Because of you, I know how to love completely, without being loved completely love in return.

Pink Floyd is only good when you're high and I don't smoke weed

He texted "Thank you for not letting me cheat 😗"

I'm his bye bye Ms. American Pie pin up girl.

He's my fast and furious almost-crashed-my-car-at-Five-Guys Khalil Beschir.

He left for home,

lyrics by Rashid Nakhle tingling up his spine.

He met his whole world after he went back home...

His whole world after he met me, obviously,

his previous whole world.

But that's fine,

I was born skeptic even of my mother's milk.

Now I'm just the tick he can't shake outta his fur, the whore of a hound dog, and he doesn't want to.

He likes the dirtiness of it, the filth.

A parasite sucking blood hidden under thick, mounds of manged fur.

I took his advice,

and listened to the first album by

Pink Floyd

I thought it was shit.

A Cross, The Sea

He'll never love me as much as he loves God.

He asked Jesus to be his Valentine,

And I'm a jealous woman.

I had a lover's rosary once and it hung around my bedpost,

But I've lost it since.

I sorted through all the sewing machines, spoiled fruit, and thimbles,

in the street bins of Oxford, England.

The filth clinging to your memory like a koala,

Squeezing blood from your arms until they

POP!!!

Laughing as the humerus

Inevitably shatters in her

Hard candy grip.

I had a lover's rosary once and it hung around my bedpost, but

I've lost it since.

Jesus offers undying

Love.

Forgiveness.

Eternal peace.

Eternal life.

A girl like me can't compete against salvation.

God help me.

Meemee's House

Every summer there I'd go,

And help her make sweet corn pone.

And on the porch we'd snap green beans,

Mosquitoes kept out by porch's screens.

We'd sit outside on rainy days,

Let her reminisce about old days.

Drink tea and while the turntable spins Pavarotti,

Make fun of church women's hats, Lord, How gaudy!

Salted watermelon, honeysuckle, and crab, At the picnic, out in the yard out back,

On the porch, watching the stars in the pitch black.

Her sing songs and silly dancing,

Her Charlie's perfume, and a never inherited garnet ring.

The pink azaleas have been removed,

For buyer's it has been improved,

The sink is now made of chrome,

And someone else will call it home.

And someone else will call it home...

Echo

I catered as a flame for a moth once,

I didn't have a choice.

She stayed silent as she flittered against my embers,

The powder from her wings burning and swirling up like cigarette smoke,

As she attempted to land on the lit wick.

I never meant to singe her,

I dimmed to try and save her,

Almost snuffing out myself.

But

The moth would fly to the ember

It's wings beating narcissus petals,

Seething soot in self-immolation.

The Chocolate Bunny

Children's laughter chimes,

Silver foil peels back,

The crimson ribbon pulled in anti-philanthropy,

Revealing the gentle creature,

Molded to sweet dark candy,

Stuck with a ludicrous smile,

For its untimely demise and violation.

Each child breaks off,

Chunks at a time.

Soon the smile is consumed,

Hollow core, the only leftover,

The last piece was taken.

The children wiped the sweet smudges,

Adorning their pudgy faces,

Savagely licking their fingers clean,

Sharing their condolences:

"That was delicious!

Too bad there wasn't more..."

Navajo and Letting Go

I snuggled the teddy bear and finished the jar of Tupelo honey

I was going to gift you for Christmas,

And I was searching for a whale bone

Whale fluke necklace to give you

after you gave yours in the Giveaway Ceremony.

I still feel you warming my towel,

And my texts that Hachikou-ed for a reply.

I pushed your boat out to sea.

But you didn't try to swim back.

You just let it carry you further to sea,

And I knew you would.

You'll ever know of these gifts,

that remain ungiven.

I've starved the wrong wolf.

One-offs

I tasted of chaos and it dripped from my tongue and

Poisoned your mouth with penny drops and dreadfuls.

"I love you" after sex, a fawn stumbling in a graveyard.

Wine words.

Intoxication touch.

Your lust tangles you my fishnets and catches you flopping like a sardine, flicking silver to get tail.

Stab your own heart with the stilettos.

Scratch the wood with

coffin nails glued tight in death red.

It's like wondering who locked the door

when you know damn well you have the key.

The moon is just a reflection of the sun,

And we shrunk before the heat even grazed us.

The Crow on St. Aldates

The kettle black crow

Pops and clicks

Between the cobblestone

For stray morsels then

With a screech—

Beside St. Aldates,

Flew like soot

At the toll of the bell.

Nest and Nectar

The hummingbird smothers me with ivy,

But she didn't care I was alive until I met the crow on St. Aldates.

She plucks shiny trash which previously adorned her nest,

And places it on my mantle,

To declutter her own.

My poor mourning dove is dead,

Her love leaves a taste reminiscent of honeysuckle.

The nectar sucked out from our lips,

Tender wings flitting

Against my arm to comfort me at the picnic table

With strewn salted watermelon and lime fun pops.

The honeysuckle bush was removed a long time ago on the backyard fence by the chinaberry tree.

That hummingbird tried to make a home here,

But she was years too late.

The Unicorn

The horn is where the magic lies.

However detached, the wish

is unfulfilled.

The is concept simple,

A horse appendaged with horn,

But the fascination continues.

Men's wonder and desire,

it is the purity they seek:

To deflower, To tarnish,

The unblemished virgin, in soft silver,

And conquer as man will conquer.

Each man convinced he will

Be the one to tame the Unicorn, and if not tame,

Then use and if not use,

Then abuse, and if not abuse,

Slay for its insubordination.

It is the same goddamn golden, unquestioned compass that

Leads the men, gaudy in their conquests, and betrays the Unicorn

laid hidden behind the cascading waterworks.

Dewdrops drip down her

Muzzle, as the golden bridle

Is implanted.

Irremovable.

She is nothing

More than a collection piece.

The Burning of Notre Dame

The bells ceased to bellow,

As they shook the hymns from their bronze skirts to save them.

Jean-Marie melts in the Hell's fire that burns the Notre Dame.

The wings of dying angels smoke

The foundation of limestone.

Empires fall.

Cathedrals burn.

And the world turns with forgotten whispers.

They speak of ice.

Will the chill come from the four winds to gather His elect?

They speak of fire.

But the demise is far more gentle.

It burns quietly like a thief in the night.

Playground Love

The chair-o-plane's chains are tangled together,

The fog has settled in the loops of chain.

The ferris wheel stands like a sentinel,

Freed from its iron bondage

From the sheer weight of

Watching over what remains.

Half the tracks are missing from

The corkscrew but it always managed

To curl up on itself without support.

The teacups no longer twirl the way

My stomach did.

Laying on the bathroom floor before I

finally hurl to purge whatever's poisoned me.

The rust, the creaking and groaning.

Sharp shrapnel jutting up.

Graffiti smeared across what's

Left of a half self-respecting water slide.

The basswood horses bob to the beat

Of a familiar childhood lullaby.

The bulbs burnt out black,

the mirrors have no reflection.

I still candy-apple hum to the spinning tune

But I won't ride the carousel again with you.

La Douleur Exquise

I would slide back shadowed sheets,

And welcome where his fingers wandered,

The chronic fever of madness drawing heat,

My body willing him to conquer.

I see the band on his hand, "make him stray,"

But my taught boundaries tip toe tilt over the edge but not too far.

I grip in white chiffon ruffles begging myself to behave,

Its sheerness marred by the tail of a cigar.

I'm carnivorous, I'd strip his bones clean,

My teeth hooking and ripping his tendons and muscle,

My eyes flashing mean and citrine,

Slits and fish nets in a cherry red tussle.

Give me what I want: a nail, a fuck, a screw.

Dirty, filthy, carnal lust, just let me pretend I'm fucking you.

I am porcupine

She nests right beneath my bristles,

Dumping powder from her wings into my pores.

Have you heard a moth scream?

It's in a hertz only I can hear and

It raises goose bumps and curdles in a hot summer's day.

The furniture owns the house but graciously provides walkways
between boxes of yesterday and one day soon.

She's the reason my words don't vomit out.

I stay alive through bristles

And silence.

Her wings beat out gunshots that echo in the woods.

Black Thumb

Your spine is a tin roof for the rain

It pins and needles at the grain

Of your wood, burnt in

charcoal smeared against the skin.

The phelgm mucks up your mind.

The bark here is rough and it stands guard over the slab,

cold and dead, like your once hungry eyes

At salted watermelon on the picnic table out back

Near the garden where she couldn't get anything to grow.

The carcasses of grief hang from a cork board.

A collage of what's gone and lost.

The last lick of a bahama mama dripping down into the horizon

Until it's consumed

Hollow as the night,

And still.

The Eastern lubbers would hiss.

Their streaks of red dragging across the sidewalk, littering the yard,

creeping slow like grumpy old men with their walkers

into her half-dead azaleas.

No Mo' Old Town Road

We suffer in the mundane

Life is the bags under our eyes

Drooping into our next cup of coffee,

The last drudges: dreams deferred to a later date or kicked out on the street to delusion some other mind.

We trudge to known outposts,

Our brown horse promotions and our pistols rapid fire data entries.

The howls of coyotes kill the sheep and fear keeps us in town as the sheriff side-eyes burning brush.

So I keep my head down and the

ivy in my skull infests every crevice,

Squeezing out what's left of polished cowbells.

We live with guns pressed against our heads,

Begging for someone else to pull the trigger.

Death of the Smalltown Mindset

Because you no longer care if you have the best potato salad

At the Wednesday Church supper.

Because your father was a military man and flew you to Germany,

And there, you gained a curious tongue.

Because that curious tongue is minoring in Linguistics,

And taught itself Ethiopian cuisine.

Because your mother is at home in Georgia,

Because here you are alone.

Because the Spanish moss and kudzu here

Festers and curls around your trachea.

Because your increased curiosity made you ask questions,

Because the Bible didn't always make sense.

So you asked questions the adults would rather you not have asked,

66

That made the children at VBS call you a devil child.

Because they beat you bloody against the pews.

Because when you gazed into Iceland's Blue Lagoon,

You saw yourself in the steam.

Because of all these things you are no longer satisfied,

With dying 18 miles from where you were born.

My Eyes Were Watching God

God, did you laugh

At the joke I made about the guy who hit the bear?

"Only YOU can prevent motor vehicle accidents."

That one was pretty funny.

And have you seen me in the pearls on Heaven's gate like I see

you in the rainbow in an oil spill's puddle?

Does my soul shine there with blinding iridescence too?

Or have you heard my voice in "How Great Thou Art" as I hear Yours

in the overtones when the church choir sings?

Did you see me boogie down to that same hymn at the age of 4

in between the pews at church,

Between the smiles and approval of the churchwomen?

You hold my sister's hand

and take her blasting off to the stars in rockets she will build.

Have You realized I'm stuck in my tiny tendon of the universe?

Head down in a cubicle,

Waiting, Watching, Writing.

I'd waited for Your message for 19 years and no answer came but

"Pomp and Circumstance" while forcing me to sing my testimony

in unfinished lyrics at her grave.

I have celebrated life through 2lbs of crab legs,

That were promised the coming summer

That was never spent with her.

But my stomach is empty,

It stays empty.

But He made me perfect.

I've echoed in the chapel's hall

as the VBS kids beat me against the pews

for asking questions I wasn't supposed to ask.

But He made me perfect,

In the way I shake without

air because I forgot

To clean the stove and I

was afraid my dad would yell at

me but I didn't mean to forget and

I write things down to remember but I can't even seem to

remember to look at what I wrote and

I want to be perfect but

God made me perfect

In the way I cry over spilled communion wine,

over everything, over nothing,

the sacramental wafer's dust in my foundation, and psalms in my

concealer.

I am sin.

I am the devil's child.

And without knowing why,

I am the woman whose name was writ in hell's fire.

And I was snuffed out between the Church's index finger and God's
thumb

Made in the USA
Coppell, TX
21 May 2020